WRITINGS FROM A
CROWDED MIND

GERMANUEL B. LEA, JR

ELEAT PUBLISHING, LLC

WRITINGS FROM A
CROWDED MIND

WRITINGS FROM A
CROWDED MIND

POEMS

JUST A FEW THOUGHTS — 6

THOUGHTS FROM A CROWDED MIND — 7

THE DAWN OF MY LIFE — 8

MAN — 10

REMEMBRANCE — 11

A VISION — 12

THE FLOWERS OF AFRICA — 13

WOMAN CHILD — 14

EMOTIONAL — 16

LENDING AN EAR — 17

LADY JOANNE — 19

UNREQUITED LOVE — 20

IDENTIFIED — 21

DELIBERATION — 22

SUNFLOWER — 24

AND I LOVE HER — 26

JOHNNIE CAN'T READ — 27

846 — 29

THOSE DAMN CHAINS — 31

THE DIVIDERS   33

A BABY'S WITHDRAWAL   35

ODE TO THE DEALERS   36

40 OUNCES AND A PRAYER   38

THE RAPIST MAN   40

BEING AN IDEA   41

IS GOD LAUGHING   42

LADY B   44

ABOUT THE AUTHOR   46

DEDICATION

This book is dedicated to my mother, Ruth M. Lea, who passed away 3 & 1/2 years ago. We often spoke of writing books together. It was her dream to become a published author. Before she passed, she worked on her autobiography with my wife, Rev. Dr. Laura Lea.

I would like to also give a special thanks to my aunt, Annie P. Thomas. She found the original writing of "Those Damn Chains" and told me I should be writing books. Well, auntie, I heard you. Also to my youngest son, Germanuel B. Lea, III and his friend, Thomas Kneeland, who walked me through to this finished product.

JUST A FEW THOUGHTS

It is dawn and I've awakened
to the rays of the early morning sun.
And as the sun rises, I take pen
and paper in hand and sit down
to write just a few thoughts—
A few thoughts about Love and
Friendship and Hate—
A few thoughts about Life and Death
and the Demise of the Human Race—
A few things about Nature, and the Heavens
on high, and the Living Things between Earth and Sky.
Dusk approaches and the horizon is a glowing orange ball.
It has crossed the Sky and nears the end of its journey.
Preparing for the Rise tomorrow again.
My Thoughts are Racing and I am so Tired,
I believe I'll rest from my Day's Journey for a while.
Like the morning sun, I, too, will rise, bathed in it's
Warmth and Glow to fill more papers with Just a Few Thoughts.

THOUGHTS FROM A CROWDED MIND

My mind is clouded with ideas and thoughts.
Which should I free, and which should I leave caught?
Should I express anger, love or loss?
Should I pen hatred, disdain or remorse?
Can I ink elation mixed with pain,
or type seduction and some heartfelt shame?
Can it be about me, or should it be about you?
Or perhaps someone else, with an alternative view.
My mind is clouded with ideas and thoughts.
which should I free, and which should I leave caught?

THE DAWN OF MY LIFE

I've stood in the shadows of despair,
now I stand in the rays of Hope
from the rising Son.

Before me on the table of Life lay
DELIVERANCE and my CAPTIVITY
all calling my name, Beckoning me
to SUNSHINE or SHADOW.

I know and understand the shadows.
I've lived in their CHILLS and peaked
from its Foggy Darkness and bathed
in it's FALSE ray of HOPE.
And I've spiraled head first into its
UNENDING BLEAKNESS, that
calls itself a JOYOUS LIFE .

I have been a PRISONER of its
self satisfaction, a GUEST of its
unending party, and a VICTIM of
its false security—

a STUMBLER in its misguided steps,
an EMPTY vessel in the warmth of its COLDNESS.

But from somewhere in the DARKNESS
there appears a RAY of HOPE—

A TINY glimmer of warmth and light, amidst the
indifferent Darkness. And I've Lifted
my eyes and raised my hands,
REACHING for the aura of the SON,

trying DESPERATELY to regain my HOPE,
striving to swim from the sea of CAPTIVITY,

//

stretching for the BEACH of DELIVERANCE
where I can BASK in the SON'S rays of HOPE.

MAN

Man, the Thorn in nature's side,
the perfect creation gone Amok—
Armed with the best tools for survival,
granted Reasoning and Understanding.
Yet, driven incoherent by Greed, Lust,
and Irrational Rationality.

Aware of himself, and his Goals,
and often nothing else. A Being
creating by destroying Creation.
Improving his existence while
mutilating the existing.

Providing for Himself while ruining
the Provisions of Nature.
In his stride to Security he creates
Insecurities. To build his Dreams
he wastes the Gifts of Nature.
In Birthing his domain he
creates Imbalances in Nature.

To live he Kills, Contaminates
and Eradicates. Nature Rebels ,
her streams stand Stagnant, her
rivers Dry Up , and her skies cry
Acid Rain and once Fertile lands
become Barren.

the Polluted seas rise as
the ice caps melt ,
Nature Struggles to Survive
with the Perfect Creation, Gone Amok.

REMEMBRANCE

Each man seeks to make his mark
upon the world. He wants a remembrance
that will stand and continue, in other men's
minds, long after he is gone—
something that says *I was here.*

There are those who mark their time
in celluloid and are remembered for
their ability to Pretend. There are those
whose voices are captured and engraved
on discs, ribbons and wax, that repeatedly
play in our ears.

There are those who are remembered in
print, as their names flash across the country's
front pages, for famous or infamous deeds of value.

Then there are those whose remembrance lives
in the heart of his fellow man and the faces
of his children. The worlds of celluloid, discs,
ribbons and print never find them, for their
greatness lives in the kindness to those about them.
They can speak with the intelligent and the illiterate,
the aristocrat and the commoner,
and no one misunderstands them.

They are carried in the hearts and minds
of family and friends. Their names invoke
laughter and storytelling. There will be no
fanfare, no jubilant televised celebrations.
but there *will* be a remembrance.

A VISION

Under the cover of darkness,
amid the deep entrancing folds of sleep.
In a land between wakefulness
and drowsiness, you once more belong to me.
In a light of dazzling orange,
or in a shroud of grayist mist,
covered by the haze of seclusion.
Adhering to the images created
by the desires of the mind, you return to me.
Once more I know the warmth
of your being, the tender look
of love, beams from your eyes to my mind.
The sweet and tantalizing taste
of your kisses are upon my lips,
warming my entire being.
The fragrant perfume of your
womanly being fills my senses.
As we climb towards the utopia
of total fulfillment, I awake,
amidst tangled sheets
and crumpled pillows.
Finding myself alone
in our bedroom.
Surrounded by the fading
fragrance of your perfume
and the memories of our Love.

THE FLOWERS OF AFRICA

Hail to the Flowers Of Africa,
who have blossomed into fertile
loveliness in a strange land.
Upon your faces appears
the symmetry of the world,
as your forebearers were slaves
to the world. Through that bondage,
your serene beauty and captivating charm,
and your ultimate womanliness,
was sought and known by all.
Your favors have been pursued
by Kings and Paupers, treasured
by Aristocrats and Commoners.
Your enchanting beauty crossed
oceans and made slaves out of slavers,
who desired your beauty. At the root
of your being is the mother of all
men, the creation of nations and
the downfall of kingdoms.
Your colors range from the fairest
of fair, to the blackest of black.
Your eyes are almonds, pears,
and ovals, twinkling as the light
of the stars. Your hair may be short
primordial curls or cascading mane.
Your lips are as full as the life
within you or as thin as the whispering
ache of your bondage. The seeds of
your ancestors were pollinated
by the world—thus, there is a
beauty about you that the
world can not resist.

WOMAN CHILD

Her skin is the color of light
honey, creamy and glowing.
Her lips process a delicate
fullness, that speaks of an inner
sweetness that has yet to be discovered
by man. Her eyes are light brown misty
pools of joy and sadness that hide
and, yet, project the troubles of her mind.
Her breasts are dainty and inviting
to the eye, and a pleasurable thought
to the mind of man. They are like twin
roses at the height of blossoming.
Her waist is small and inspires a man
to want to embrace her, and to know her
intimately. Her hips are full, tapering into
smooth muscular thighs, which flow into
sculptured legs and delicate feet.

She is a woman—
A woman that is luscious, desirable,
physically devastating to the eyes of man.
From her cold black hair to the tips of her toes,
she walks triumphantly
and, yet, she is humble
and unaware in her physical prison—
a prison because she is a child,
who has come into womanly fullness,
but not of age and mind—a child.
Aware of the stares of men,
she giggles and blushes in childish joy,
and in the excitement of being noticed.
Her mind can find enjoyment in the flight
of a bird, or a simple hole in the ground,

For She Is A Child.

EMOTIONAL

Swept through a sea of endless
warmth, generated by the physical
dynamo of desire, they called their
fusion *Love*. Their hands touched,
their lips met and, through that kiss,
they tasted one another.

Then, their bodies fused together
in a passionate interlude they
called *Love*. And when it was over,
there was silence, for each knew not the other;
without the language of their bodies,
they had no conversation. Lost was the verbal
expression of *Love*—
but...they loved one another?

Their minds flowed in different galaxies,
with wavering uncertainty on their relationship,
each questioning the reality of their feelings.
But...does anything exist for them beyond their physical fusion?

They wanted and desired the same things in life,
yet each of them had a different definition of importance.
Conversation was needed to fuse their thoughts,
just as Emotion had fused their bodies.

If this did not occur, all could be lost,
for Emotion is not enough.

LENDING AN EAR

A friend I met this fateful day,
           with her hair a mess, and her makeup astray.

With swollen eyes and a tear-stained face.
           Her sobbing body in my arms, she laid.

In a weeping voice, slowed by gasping breath,
           she swore that there was nothing left.

No love to build on, no trust to keep,
           no vow unbroken, no desire to entreat.

He's no good, she cried, just a selfish lout.
           He has no idea what Love is about.

He seeks to control, and not to console.
           When it comes to Love he has the sight of a mole.

I've begged and I've pleaded, I've cried and coerced.
           Hell, I'm a young woman to Love, not some tired old flirt.

Then she looked up and smiled, and her lips spoke these words:

You know it's time to quit. I'm going to take
myself home and straighten out this shit.

        If I can't straighten it out by the end of the day,
        then tonight at home in my bed alone I'll lay.
        I will rise tomorrow and start a new way.

I will place his clothes on the porch, with care,
with a note stating, You must go elsewhere.

        I will change the locks, so there's no doubt
        that this is my house, and he's been moved out.

//

I found him, I dressed him
and to my home I brought him.

      I bought the rings and made him my man,
      but tomorrow, I'll be alone again.

LADY JOANNE

Lady Joanne with the tangerine breasts,
a sweet mouthful of enjoyment, no more, no less,
with a quaff of black curls and dancing brown eyes,
chiseled legs and sculptured thighs, and a beautiful
rounded butt to attract men's eyes.

A Small package of passion and lust combined,
that triggers a man's wants and manipulates his mind,
a promise of pleasure, a hint of joy,
a show of teeth with a smile so coy.

Are you to be held tenderly as a child first born,
or gripped tightly, as a woman of passionate storms?
Will your kisses be gentle and warm,
as a summer breeze, or a twirling wind before a tornado is born?

Will we share a love of passion and devoted trust,
or a scalding affair of sweltering lust,
an affair of steamy days and seething nights,
with bodies rushing to climatic delights?

Lady Joanne who brings me such elation,
a woman who has captured my
thoughts and elevated my sensations.
Will I be your forever love,
or just another way station?

UNREQUITED LOVE

There is a LOVE, which is eternally
unspoken, and can never be acted upon.
A Love between two people, who can
never come together: IT'S an UNREQUITED LOVE.

It's a passion unsatisfied, a desire unfilled.
For the sake of others, It must remain a LOVE denied—
A LOVE shackled in their hearts and minds,
ignited by chance meetings.

Meetings in which only eyes may glance carefully.
And hands may touch in cheerful greetings
of *Hellos* and *Good-Byes*.

Though fingertips burn with passion,
and eyes twinkle with desire,
there is a constant smoldering,
But there can be no Fire.

It is a Burden shared by Two,
a couple's dream that will never come true.
A LOVE without beginning and yet a LOVE at it's end.
A LOVE that is Known in two hearts, but is never in view.

It is an UNREQUITED LOVE.

IDENTIFIED

I stand at the crossroads of life, with little to offer, and less being offered to me. My past is dark and dreary, cast in dimly lit shadows of darkness and light. And always there is a force Lording over me.

I am a descendant of Kings and Queens, I have been both servant and master. I have been both Praised and Ignored. I have been Chained and somewhat Freed. I am a person of two continents—one, my ancestral home and, the other, built on the backs of my ancestors. One I only know of, the other I live *in*, amidst the shame of racism, the brutality of hatred and the fear of humiliation, along with a "justifiable" wrongful death. I have been enslaved both mentally and physically, I have over achieved, while being undereducated. I have been a hero in war and the cause of war, and a hostage in a nation of freedom. I'm considered both an embarrassment and an honor to my country.

Who am I?

I am a Black Man in America.

DELIBERATION

We are here from the bowels of Deliberation,
once our enslavers sat with our captors,
deliberating the price of our captivity—
haggling over the value of our ancestors
in the cost of knives, beads, guns and assorted trinkets—
deliberately singled out by their enemies
to be removed from their homeland
and rendered into slavery—
to be ground into submissiveness
and whipped into obedience—
manacled to a society that stripped
them of their identity and erased their pride.

Our ancestors became valued by the strength
of their backs and the wealth of their loins.
In the midst of society, a Deliberation arose.

Is it right that one man should own another?
Is it right for him to brand him and work him
like an animal of the fields?
Is it right that one man can treat
another man as if, he is no man at all—
even buy, sell, and trade them like prized livestock?

The answer was decreed *NO*, and a Nation moved
from Deliberation to Separation.

Then, the volleys of opinions spawned
the thunder of cannon, and the crackle of rifle
fire, and the slashing of bayonet thru flesh,
as brother fought brother and fathers faced sons,
and friends died at the hands of friends.

In the end, our ancestors were declared to be free,
but their fate fell under new laws by both

//

winner and loser, and they became the lost.
The truth of justice was and *is* often guided by
the COLOR of man.

The invisible shackles of law and self-righteousness
imprisoned our ancestors and, now, imprison us.
In a first-rate country, *WE* are its second-rate citizens,
and in the Halls of Congress both STATE and FEDERAL,
OUR presence is being DELIBERATED. Through wars
and battle actions, through science and education,
we have earned accolades, awards, and reverence.
But, as of yet, we have not been totally accepted,
nor our personage as Citizens recognized.

In essence, we are still being Deliberated,
as the echoes of the past move forward,
and the laws are adjusted, to perhaps enforce
the OLD Prejudices under a so-called New Enlightenment,
as the designs for man with man are pursued with all Deliberate Haste.

SUNFLOWER

She was first in the field and grew quickly.
Straight and tall she grew, ever reaching for the sun.
The field mouse, the cricket, and the toad, loved her
as they watched her buds turn to blooms.

The bees came to sip of her nectar
and carry away her pollen. The spider
spun a silken web amidst her branches.
The aphids dwelt among her leaves.
She was the provider of home and food for many.

In the glory of the sun she stood,
wavering in the gentle summer breeze,
drinking nightly from the dewy moisture
of the earth, and bathing in the summer rain.

In the scheme of things, as seasons fell
into seasons, she felt the pangs of change.
The aphids perished in the early frost,
and the bees came no more.

For her flowers had become discs
of brown dryness. The cricket sang
no more, and the winter winds tore
the spider's web from her branches.

And the field mouse sought a warmer
winter home. And the sap of life ceased
to rush through her limbs.

Her coffin was the forest floor,
with its covering of wet leaves and moss.
Her casket walls were the tall trees
reaching skyward. It's lid, the sky
sprinkled with an inkling of stars.

//

And in the midst of this sorrow,
the clouds cried, and the moon hid
in their shadows. At the midnight hour,
the animals of the forest gathered about her,
and carefully covered her body.

Using the fallen leaves and twigs
and broken branches, they gathered
with tear-stained faces.

With the coming of sunrise, a mist
covered the forest, and the dew fell
like tear drops upon the forest floor.
The birds sang a Hymn of Sorrow,
and the sun hid behind the clouds,
as all of nature paid homage
to the Death of a Sunflower.

AND I LOVE HER

Her beauty is undeniable, her charm
is overwhelming. Like an unending dream
she roams through my mind. In times of hurt,
in times of loneliness, in times of love lost,
I would love her, but she calls for me, her *friend*.

A crown of flowing black tresses atop an oval face,
with slightly almond shaped eyes, and thin kissable lips,
which speak of passion. She nestles her head in my chest,
over my heart.

She says, "Thanks, my friend, for being here for me."
Yet I could Love Her wonderfully full breast, rising and falling
in the anguish of lovelessness—

A tapered waistline, flaring to full hips,
and perfectly aligned thighs and legs,
which dance in my heart, and elate my being.
She snuggles close, as if in her father's
arms; Tho I would Love her.

She has always chosen those who would use her,
abuse her, and taste of her sweetness and leave her
crying for the rain of love to fall upon her.
And when her hurts swell in her heart,
and misery moves beyond containment,
and the tears of sorrow flow,
She calls for me, her *friend*.

I run to answer her call, to bring her that
which is missing. To bring unto her compassion,
an understanding tenderness, with a warm,
loving embrace. I hold her, shielding the Love
I feel for her. She sighs, nestles in my arms,
kisses my cheek and says, "Thank you, my friend."

JOHNNIE CAN'T READ

He was a star and earth bound
comet passing through the system.

Yet, he did not understand he was
a victim of his own abilities.
A victim being systematically
passed on, for the glory of others.
He was the man on campus,
Its luminary of distinction.
They cheered for him, they raved
about him, they raved about him,
and as we say: They gave him His Props
and the system passed him on.

His times on the oval track were unbelievable.
His batting average soared. His assists, rebounds,
and points per game were always in double figures.
But, Johnnie didn't understand math—

his name, forever in their Historical Archives—
a Legend forever imprinted in the school record books.
But, Johnnie didn't like nor understand History.

He was spoken of and written of as a
Present and Future superstar, who would perhaps
be a Hall of Famer. But because Johnnie can't Read,
he listened to the words, soaked up the Praise,
and was guaranteed a passing grade,
because he was Johnnie Superstar,
the school's Sports Idol.

The system maximized his physical abilities, and
minimized his understanding, never educating
him above failure.

//

His Diploma says High School Graduate,
His SATs say fifth grade education,
The doors of the colleges close before Him.
Their system does not allow them to open the
portal to His foreseen Destiny. Although his
physical abilities are welcomed, his lack of
understanding keeps the doors closed.

Hence, another star is burned out,
and a rising Star is snared by the
gravity of Learning.

Pulled to earth with a thud
and a semi-silent crash,
his remains scattered amongst
the fields of the functional illiterates—

Because, Johnnie Can't Read.

846

8 Minutes & 46 SECONDS,
How long can it be?

For George Floyd it was
a LifeTime, spent under a Knee.

His hands cuffed behind him,
His face to the street.

Imprints of the concrete
pressed into his cheek.

And a Knee on his NECK.

He had peacefully surrendered,
He'd given no strife.

He was thinking that surely
this would save his Life.

He knew not the executioner
was among the four.

Someone who cared not
for Floyd's Life, But the Badge he still wore.

In the cowardly action, He was taking great pride.
Showing great power and strength
over a man Penned and Bound—
A man who could not Fight Back.

The crowd watched in Horror and Stunned Disbelief,
as the Pressure applied caused Floyd such Grief.

//

Once again He Surrendered, thinking this strife
should end, and from His Despair find some Relief.
Perhaps he would remove His Knee, so he could receive fresh air.
With a clouded mind and weakened voice,
Hoarsely, he Uttered "I CAN'T BREATHE, I CAN'T BREATHE."

His words fell on Deaf ears, and the Pressure increased.
He now knew that death would be His only Relief.
It was Comfort He needed, so that
He might move on in Peace.
So He Called for his Mother, For He knew
in Her arms He would find Sweet Release.

He Gasped one more time, this time without stress.
He Surrendered His Life, and Mother welcomed Him to rest.
Now a Nation Watched in Stunned Disbelief,
for they had Just Watched a Killing on NATIONWIDE TV.

8 Minutes & 46 SECONDS, HOW LONG CAN IT BE?
For George Floyd it was a LIFETIME, spent under a KNEE,
His hands cuffed behind Him, His Face to the Street,
IMPRINTS of the CONCRETE , PRESSED in HIS CHEEK,

With a KNEE ON HIS NECK.

THOSE DAMN CHAINS

The wind was blowing briskly, and the old chains hanging from the fence chimed mournfully. I saw a change come over the old man, as he listened to the sound. He stopped rocking and calmly looked straight at me and smiled, saying,

> *"Son, listen to the sound of those chains. That sound has followed me for the better part of my life. Once I was a proud young man, a fledgling warrior, coming into manhood, until I was reduced to a mere lump of flesh, by those Damn Chains. My place in life was reduced to that of a peasant, a beggar, but I was even less than that—I was a Slave. And my degradation began when I was shackled with those Damn Chains. I was quick and eager to learn, for I was taught early that rebellion only brought pain. First, the bite of the whip, and confinement in a place no bigger than a woodbox, where the sun beat down mercilessly and gradually cooked your brains. And during all that time, I was shackled by those Damn Chains. I soon gave up trying to walk as a man, and began to shuffle along, with each step controlled by the width of my Damn Chains. With shoulders slumped and head bowed, I soon learned to do a Niggers bidding. Then I received my reward, the removal of those Damn Chains. But I had clasped a tighter set of chains upon my being—the Chains of submission, blind obedience, and defeat. I resigned myself to be less than a Man so I could survive, to be walked on, spat on, and examined like a prized animal—to be treated worse than a humble jackass. You know, it all began with those Damn Chains."*

He paused for a moment and smiled, then he said: "Boy, you know they say we free a free people now. They fought a war to free us. We are supposed to be able to go where we want and everything, but you know most of us are still Slaves in our minds. Slaves, because we don't know where to go or what to do. 'Cause Master always told us that. You know boy, most of our people are still here doing the Master's bidding. Hell, we've forgotten or never knew what it means to be free. We still in those DAMN CHAINS, whether they are real or invisible."

//

After he said that, he resumed rocking as if nothing had happened or a thing said; he was once again lost deep within himself. The rhythm of his rocking seemed to be in time with the off-beat melody played by the wind-blown Chains.

I thought about the last few things he had said, about us always being Slaves, and Prayed it was just the PRATTLINGS of an Old Man. An Old Man who had suffered unendingly for most of His Life. Two days later, He died. I BUILT HIM A NICE PINE COFFIN FOR HIS FINAL RESTING PLACE, and buried him. And in His Coffin, I placed those DAMN CHAINS.

THE DIVIDERS

We are the bastions of racial Disharmony.
The hands and feet of the Problems,
the Tongue and Teeth of Disruption.
We prevent humanity from Mixing
and Blending together, as a truly
functional Society—

A society built on the Foundation of
LOVE, HUMILITY, PEACE and EQUALITY.
We keep them separate and in Turmoil,
so that UNREST reigns.

We Create mistrust within and without;
there is no one who avoids our Shadows of Doubt.
We speak with conviction, we lie with ease,
the Truth is only, what we say it is.

We allow no Peace, and Disdain brotherly Love,
If you are not of our race, you're not quite a man.
We are the weapons of the army of Hatred,
the tools of the mechanics of Unrest.

We are the Machinery for the
Farmers of Self Serving Aggression.
We are the Ink in the Pens of
Selfish Self-Serving Righteousness.

If we were WRESTLERS, we would
be Tag Team Champions. If we were Golfers,
we would always be at the Top of the tour.
If we were Baseball or Football or Basketball
players, we would be Perennial Allstars.

WE are the Dividers of Society, the Building
Blocks for the Walls of Separation.

//

The PROMOTERS of Racism, the
Mortar for the walls of Inequality.
Without Us, there would be no
Social Unrest, Hatred, Injustice
and the Solid Conviction of
Self Righteousness.

Without Us, All Men Could Live As Brothers.
Peace would be a Constant presence, and Equality
would Trample Racism and Bigotry into NON-EXISTENCE.
For We are FEAR, HATRED, GREED, EGOTISM,
IGNORANCE and HYPOCRISY.

A BABY'S WITHDRAWAL

I have no concept of time and space,
I have no awareness of who I am,
Nor who I may become.

But I know I am to be someone somewhere.
I feel tortured, I'm racked with pain and seem
to have needs I don't understand. Sometimes I lay
twitching, my nerves all aflame.

Then I lay crying and screaming,
from this HELL that I'm in.
I'm tenderly touched, I'm comfortingly held.
I'm sung to and prayed for, that I might find rest.
There's this person who holds me and continually
cries aloud,

"O Lord please forgive me of my
sins against this child. This child,
who is withdrawing from the DRUGS
that I took. This Child who must get off
the DRUGS I took. This child who's unaware it's
a FIX he needs. A FIX to calm him,
relax him and place him at ease.

My days are just beginning,
perhaps I'll find peace.
But, for now I'll be crying,
to express my grief.

I'm too young to look forward,
and too new to look back.
I'm just a NEW BORN BABY,
strung out on CRACK.

ODE TO THE DEALERS

Here's to the Dealers, both White and Black,
who rise to riches on poor dreamers' backs—
Who offer up pleasures to release
the mind of a stressful life, which often
creates personal and internal strife.

They are the suppliers and pushers of
this so-called relief—who stress there's
no harm in tasting their wares, and
just for a moment, forgetting all of your cares.

They are the hustlers of whores
and the sellers of smack—
The dealers of Heroin,
Cocaine and Crack—
The destroyers of morals, the
ruiners of home and family life—
The reasons for the loss of Husbands,
Wives, Sons, Daughters and LIFE—
The Pied Pipers of Social Decay
marching to Wealth.

Their sales make no difference, from child
to adult, even nickels, dimes, and pennies
can help pay the cost.

From the Penthouse to the Poorhouse,
their customers come; Most have Lost their
identity and just Users they become.

//

Their habitual purchases grow more Frequently,
and their weekend habits are now Daily need—
a Need the Dealers KNOW will bring them much
cash, because the Casual User now has a Monkey
on His back—A Monkey that grows with each Snort,
each Shot, and each Inhalation, giving the Dealers
a Cash Elevation.

So here's to the Dealers both Black and White,
who Hustle the street corners both Day and Night—
who sell joy for a moment and perhaps Enslavement for Life—
who push Death and Ruination, Trouble and Strife, and
reap the Cream of Success from the Sorrows of Life.

40 OUNCES AND A PRAYER

The empty bottle lay at my feet
and many others littered the street.
It was a 40-ounce brand, who cares?
Just another nail in the coffin
of a Soul in despair.

I remembered the long and
sleepless nights—Nights spent Drinking
and Smoking and looking for Insight.
Mom had taught me to Pray at the end
of each day, so with no conviction,
my prayers I would say. I remember
thinking that no one cared,
that all I needed was a Joint,
40 ounces and a hollow prayer.

To admit I was lost, I did not dare,
for it would cost me my friends,
who shared my despair.
Then one night at a Revival, the Spirit
fell on me, a new Insight came calling
to help set me free. It showed me that
Smoke and Drink were really my
Ball and Chain—they solved no Problems
and Cured no Pains, but sometimes they
were the Problems I needed to Change.

So now each Day begins and ends
with a meaningful prayer, Thanking God
for His Loving Care. My problems seem
to Fade away, as I Lean on Jesus to
Find My Way.

His messages hold truth, His words
lift despair, whatever my needs are,

//

 I've found in His Care.
Artificial Stimulation, I need to
Smoke no more. My troubled Thirst
is Quenched, by the Scriptures
I Read and Quote. The Joints and
40 ounces share my table no more,
and I shed tears of Joy when my
Knees touch the floor in Meaningful Prayers.

THE RAPIST MAN

For the life of me, I can't understand what goes through the mind of the Rapist Man. How can there be a peaceful, loving sexual satisfaction, amidst the terror of his violent actions? What type of gratification can be conceived from a woman who's crying and screaming and offering up pleas? What good is so-called Love obtained in strife, using the barrel of a gun or the point of a knife?

How can someone feel so well pleased after fighting open, clenched thighs, crossed legs and tight knees, knowing there can be no pleasure or bliss, when you are warding off scratches and bites, instead of tasting an inspired kiss?

Now at that climatic moment, when passion and desire meet in volcanic eruptions and trembling sensations—when you are catapulted into a state of near unconsciousness—where must his mind be? Because for the sake of control, this moment must elude him for the sake of control. So, for the life of me, I can't understand what goes through the mind of the Rapist Man.

BEING AN IDEA

I am a universal traveler—
I am tied to no beginning
and uncertain of my ending.
My highway is vast and crosses
unending intersections with sideroads
to various destinations.

I am bound to nothing—
gravity can put no hold on me.
I am free to travel the vastness
of the mind. I may become universal
or remain only personal.
My presence is unusual and, yet,
normal to everyone.

I can be felt, but not seen.
I can be visualized, but not heard.
I can become a reality, after being a thought.
I can be a success after being a failure,
or perhaps a failure, before I'm a success.
I am a part of every being, I am often
shared amongst others.

I am the driving force behind a creation.
But, you must remember that I am, and
I am always different and yet often the same.
And sometimes, for the sake of fear
or the lack of courage, I remain unborn
and, yet, I still am—

For I am an Idea, and I will
always be in the mind of mind.

IS GOD LAUGHING

Does God have a sense of humor?
Maybe yes, Maybe no.
Is He watching with great enjoyment
the acts of man, here below?
Does He find satisfaction in His creation,
which walks this earth, or does He ponder
and wonder what are we really worth?
He gave the ultimate sacrifice, so our sins
would be forgiven.

But, most of us spend our lives
as if there was no heaven.
He gave us earthly riches to share
amongst ourselves, and yet
we fight each other to own the lion's share.

To control the flow, to make the dollars,
to live in richness as others live in squalor.
With the earth's richest spread far and wide,
the key is to share with one another,
not to control in Hollow Pride.

As God watches all these actions
in the plight of mankind, can He
once more grant forgiveness,
and send to us a LAMB?

As man loses himself in self-serving desires,
the Spirit of GOD'S LOVE amongst man
dies as a funeral fire.

Does GOD have a sense of humor?
Maybe yes.
Maybe no.

//

Is He watching, with great Pride and
Enjoyment, the human race here below,
or is there a Frown upon His face
and sorrow in His heart,

watching the Majority of mankind
seek egotistical satisfaction and,
from God, live Apart?

Does each raindrop represent a tear
for mankind and each windstorm
a sigh for His plight?
Is there hope for tomorrow,
or do we face eternal night?

LADY B

Breonna Taylor, may you rest in Peace.
A Beautiful Black Lady, whose Life was INCOMPLETE.
With twinkling brown eyes and a beguiling smile,
with a dash of mischievousness was your personal style.
A beloved Daughter and a Loving Sister were you
and the Beloved of Kenneth, who laid beside you.

You were a woman of substance, with an embracing heart.
Known for your kindness and caring ways.
But carelessness sent you to an early grave.
The police had a warrant, called *No Knock*.
That meant, Break In, take the criminal, and
if necessary take the Shot.

Why you died in a hail of Bullets, is still a mystery.
The address was old, perhaps the warrant was too.
The criminal they sought had gone on the move.
No validations were made, no facts were checked.
They assumed it was still the home of the criminal suspect.
Next to your love you lay sleeping, at peace, in your home,
your day complete, and totally unaware of the violence to come.

A victim of circumstance, is how it's explained.
Though they broke in like criminals and startled your man.
He fired his gun in self-defense. Protecting you and your home
was his only intent. He didn't know that you all were under arrest.
Behind a bail of bullets, he heard the shout, *Police*.
But now you lay dying, under your blood-soaked sheets.
Your defenseless, bullet-riddled body, expiring fast.
There is yet no quality explanation of how this came to pass.

//

No words of sorrow or caring remorse;
Just evasive conversations, to justify your loss.
The Injustice of Justice, when a Black Life is Lost.
Another Police Incident, Another Officer in Fear,
Another defenseless Black Life that didn't have a Prayer.

ABOUT THE AUTHOR

Germanuel B. Lea Jr. was born on Aug. 29, 1947 in Columbus, Ohio to the parents of Ruth M. (Harris) Lea & Germanuel B. Lea, Sr., both deceased. Raised in East St. Louis, IL where he graduated from Lincoln Sr. High School in 1966. After being hired at Bethlehem Steel in July of 1969, he enlisted in the United States Army in January of 1970. Bethlehem granted Lea military leave during his enlistment period.

In November of 1973, Lea returned to work at Bethlehem Steel. Over a period of time, he attended the mill's Craft School and became an A-Rate Millwright. Bethlehem Steel was bought by International Steel Group (ISG), who then sold it to ArcelorMittal, from whom he retired, accredited with 43 years of continuous service. I am a father to six adult children and a grandfather to seventeen grandchildren.

He has been happily married to Rev. Dr. Laura B. Lea for the past forty-one years. Together, they now serve at Life Temple Church of God In Christ under Elder Robert Flemming, in Michigan City, IN.

www.ingramcontent.com/pod-product-compliance
Lightning Source LLC
Chambersburg PA
CBHW070014100426

42741CB00012B/3238